For These
SOULS

A trip to Haiti

ASHLEY THOMAS

iUniverse, Inc.
New York   Bloomington

For These Souls
A trip to Haiti

iUniverse books may be ordered through booksellers or by contacting:

iUniverse
1663 Liberty Drive
Bloomington, IN 47403
www.iuniverse.com
1-800-Authors (1-800-288-4677)

ISBN: 978-1-4502-7198-1 (pbk)
ISBN: 978-1-4502-7199-8 (ebk)

Printed in the United States of America

iUniverse rev. date: 11/4/2010

This book is dedicated to all of the people
that were willing to support me through this
process and is published in honor
of my Grandfather, Jim Thomas.

⌒⌒ Preface ⌒⌒

In order for my story to make sense, you first need to know the basis of my grandfather's story. Up until my uncle remarried in 2007, I was his only granddaughter. We had a very special relationship filled with love, adoration, and acceptance. We shared many things, most of which I did not even share with my parents or friends. He was my go-to guy whenever something came up or I needed a prayer partner. He was the person I hope my future husband will be like. I was close with my parents, always had been, but although they were Christians, we never really shared exactly the same sight in what a relationship with God really was. Even when I was in middle and high school, I would go to church with them, and was very involved, but I felt like something was missing. That "something" I later came to find out was the actual relationship with Christ! I had the foundation, the Biblical knowledge if you may, but I didn't have a close relationship with God. Sure I prayed and studied the Bible, but I didn't really get it. Upon leaving for college, in Michigan, it was the perfect opportunity to find a church that met my spiritual needs. My boyfriend at the time invited me to his church, and since I had already tried many others and didn't feel that that was where God wanted me, I agreed to go. From day one I was intent that that was the church I was supposed to go to, Saline First Assembly of God.

My grandfather, Jim Thomas, understood that relationship with Christ and was definitely taking full advantage of the veil being pulled down in order to allow a personal relationship with Christ. When we visited each other, either he came to Ohio or I went to Oklahoma, we would sit on the couch, holding hands, talking about God. He started early in his life and continued until he died. He did missions work across the Atlantic Ocean to numerous countries but also did missions work in the United States and in the town he lived in. My cousin Dustin, before he died, was even able to go on a missions trip with my grandfather to ___ Romania when I was in middle school. I wanted to go so badly but I had too many health problems to be allowed to go on a missions trip by my parents. At my grandfather's funeral, there was even a gentleman who gave his life to the Lord. My grandfather truly was an example of Christian love and doing the work that we as Christians were called to do.

When my grandfather died in December of 2008, I put it in my mind that I would never go on a missions trip, as it would bring up too many memories of him. If I couldn't share the experience with my grandfather, then I didn't want to go. It was a very selfish thought, but it was how I felt.

God, however, had other plans, as He usually does. A missionary from Haiti came to talk to our church congregation on a Sunday evening in September of 2009. I felt a call from God that I was supposed to go, but due to the fact that I had closed off all hopes of going on a missions trip, and because I knew financially speaking it'd never work, I put the feeling aside. Even though I had personally resolved that I was imagining the feelings, I asked a few close prayer warriors of mine to pray about it, what could it hurt? What in the world could God want me to do in Haiti? A country rarely in the news, and definitely not one of the neediest countries out there, it just did not make any sense.

In January of the same school year, a devastating earthquake hit Haiti, and more specifically Port-au-Prince. I received call after call from close friends and just acquaintances, Christians and non Christians, prayer warriors and non, people that knew about the September experience and those that did not, saying that I should go to Haiti. I froze solid. I went back a few months later, after requesting a detail description of my calls during a certain week, and had, in fact, received OVER 50 telephone calls from various people in a two day span, all of which encouraged me to go to Haiti. I do not know how many texts I received about it, but there were plenty of those as well. But let's be honest, anyone who knows me knows I am a hard headed person, and that wasn't enough convincing for me to know that it was what I was supposed to do.

I let it ride a bit, not willing to make such a financial commitment as I wasn't happy at my current place of employment and had no leads on something for the following year. God continued to show me passages in the Bible of people spreading His word, and so I started looking around, not really in search of something that I thought was actually going to happen, but just for fun. I looked up a few different places, but being an educator, I really wanted to go in the summer. I finally found one organization that had a summer trip planned, and I figured I'd email the director to see if there were any more openings and the cost etc. I received an email back, asking for more details about who I was as a person, and it was pretty much set after that. The head organizer of the trip sent me an email later on explaining the cost of the trip and

3

some other general information for the trip and I was signed up ready to go.

For something that I wasn't planning on doing, it sure was coming together nicely. I took it as God's way of showing me that He was going to make this happen. I quickly wrote up support letters and sent them out, and within days they began pouring back in. It intrigued me who donated! It was not my closest of friends and family as I figured. It was the random people that had made a difference in my life, or I had made a difference in their life at one point. It was very interesting to see who was willing to take a risk on me and who was not. It was clear that I had the support of some people, although my family was still questioning whether this was a good idea or not.

On Good Friday, of 2010, I was hit by a car while saving a little boy's life. I didn't, and still don't, consider myself a hero. I feel like I was in the right place at the right time. The mom was so thankful and in tears as she asked why I did it, and I simply explained that it was honestly just a reaction, I didn't even think about it. I went home that night, not wanting to go to the emergency room, but not feeling well, so I went to sleep at a friend's place for the evening. The pain was getting worse and worse where I was hit by the car, and when I would finally fall asleep for a few minutes, I'd wake up and throw up everywhere. After doing that three or four times, I decided it was time to go into the emergency room as the pain in my hip and the concussion was obviously worse than I originally thought.

I sat in the ER alone, for quite some time as I waited for a room and then finally waited for test results. After taking a second CT scan, a doctor came in to talk to me, asking if I had any friends or family around that we should wait for, which is when the feeling of being scared began. I felt like my stomach was empty and moving slowly downward. The doctor explained that a second CT scan was necessary because they saw a mass in the first scan. The second scan confirmed that I had had a brain tumor. Sure the concussion had some pretty bad side effects as I hit my head pretty hard since I was holding the little boy with my hands and couldn't catch myself, so my head caught all of my body weight, and my pelvic bone suffered no breaks, only some intense bone bruising, but the thing that I should be scared of is this tumor sitting in my brain. The doctor went away to let the news sink in as they debated what to do next. I decided it was time to call my parents and ask them to make the 70 minute drive up to be with me. A friend's mom even stopped by and sat with me until my parents could get there, which was the sweetest thing ever, seeing how I was a bit on the shocked and scared side.

I had gone into the ER with a bad concussion and a hurting pelvis, and now they were telling me that I had a brain tumor? It wasn't making much sense. They ran a few more tests, set up some doctors appointments for me and got me set up for a biopsy the next day. My mom got there around 11:30 at night, and I was released by about 3:30 in the morning to go home and follow up with some specialists. I still wasn't feeling well, I had to deal with the after affects of being hit by a car, and now had to deal with the "what if" game. Many different scenarios crossed my mind. I dove deeper into my Bible, when I could actually see clearly and read again, and I prayed, a lot! Never before had I wanted my grandfather available to talk on the phone with so that I could discuss this with him. I needed someone that I could talk to. I needed someone to make some sense out of it all.

I went to the doctor the next day for a biopsy, and just prayed the entire time they were doing the procedure. We were luckily on Spring Break the week that I had all of these appointments and so not much work was missed, that is the good news. I went back to work the next week, and attempted to pretend that everything was normal. My kids knew something was wrong. It was hard to hide the emotions changing rapidly or my forgetfulness, which was never a problem before. It was a secret that was eating me alive. I couldn't let anyone know because then they would know I wasn't on my "a" game, so to speak. I was frustrated and annoyed. I'd call my mom at night, crying, telling her that I hated the person that I had become due to this stupid tumor, and being a mother who is a planner and likes to think ahead, and always thought of my bests interests, she had only one piece of advice, "you should cancel your trip." Those five words I heard from more and more people as the days went on. They didn't understand the feeling that I had that God called me to take this trip! He put the idea in my head, He funded it, He alone made it happen. How could I just cancel the trip. So, I did what anyone would do, I stopped talking about the trip, because no matter who I talked to, those five words were their suggestion.

I didn't see how a God who created the earth, a God who parts seas, a God who brings the dead back to life, a God who is my Father yet my friend, could want me to do that. So I stuck to my guns, and did what I felt I needed to do. I stayed on guard with the trip. I told people that it would be okay. God didn't lead me this far to take away something that He planted in me. Everything would be fine by August, it just had to be, and I kept telling myself that. Although I walked the walk and talked the talk, sure there were times where I thought about canceling the trip, thinking that maybe this wasn't the best idea, but when I got in my prayer closet, I knew that I was supposed to go to Haiti with this group, and share God's love with these people who had lost everything and were trying to rebuild their lives. I couldn't imagine having to rebuild my life without Jesus, and I didn't want them to have to, I had made a decision to go to Haiti no matter what.

I was at a church service one Saturday night a month or two later, Carpenter's House (It's a revival center that I helped create and am fairly active in to say the least.) and Rev. Charles Kincaid prayed for me that night, for total healing in my body. I believe that night God took away the tumor! I was back in the ER later in the month for some other issues I was having with my body, yes it has been a crazy year so far, and they did some "routine" CT scans to check if the increased pressure in my spinal cord was causing problems in my brain, and came to find out that the tumor was gone! Hallelujah! God is so good! It's actually a little side note, but that doctor was so funny. I had been admitted to the hospital that night for various reasons and my neurologist came to pay me a visit at 6:30 in the morning. Now I don't know about you, but seeing how I had been in the ER since 9 am the day before, and hadn't gotten to my room until about 4 in the morning, I was not all that excited or chipper when my neurologist comes knocking on the door waking me up out of my morphine/benadryll induced sleep. He said that he had reviewed the scan and noticed that my brain tumor was gone. To which I replied "I know," and rolled back over to sleep, thinking that was all he wanted to tell me, to my amazement he KEPT ON GOING!! He told me that he had been looking over my files for the last few hours and kept coming to the same conclusion. He would look at the original CT scan where the brain tumor was present, he saw the following scans where the tumor continued to get progressively larger, and then last night's scan where the tumor was just MIA. He was in puzzlement over it. Now, had I been in a more "right" state of mind, I would have loved to explain to him how my God is bigger and better than any medicine he could offer and that He took care of it because He does not like to see His people hurting, but like previously mentioned, I was TIRED, medicated, and wanted to sleep. It just makes me laugh thinking about it because he was so astonished about the entire case. Praise God for showing science what He, and only He, can do!

So needless to say, it has been a very interesting 7 months! I leave in two weeks to go to Haiti. I could not be more excited. I am slowly but surely purchasing things that I need for my trip, and setting aside things that I don't want to forget to take. It is going to be a trip of a lifetime. I cannot wait to come back and write all about it, telling everyone what God is doing not only in Haiti, but also in Ypsilanti, Michigan!

I think my brother's response last week was my favorite. He is overseas for a year with his wife working, so a lot of our conversations have been on the phone and on a time crunch. Although from the day I told them about the trip, and the accident, and everything else going on in my life, my brother has been worried and suggested that I didn't go. But last week, we had a conversation, and it truly blessed my heart. He told me that although he was scared for me to go, that he was very proud of me for being willing to take the time and commitment to help other people in the world. He said he wished he could be like me! Can you believe that! My big brother's approval, and the thought of my Grandfather looking down on me with a smile, makes this entire journey that much more enjoyable to think about!

~It's gonna be worth it!~

⌁ Day One ⌁
Monday

12:23pm- All systems go! Brittany dropped me off at the airport, I made it through security, had some lunch, and now I'm waiting for the plane. I am excited to meet up with my team! It will be interesting to finally meet these people who I have been emailing back and forth with these past few months. I still cannot believe that God is allowing ME to go to Haiti! Holy Cow! He is so amazing!!!!

2:40pm- I've decided that people have it all wrong. It is so much better to be shorter rather than taller. I remember being in love with flying when I was a little kid, but that was before I grew my legs. These seats are so cramped. I still love taking off though. I love looking out the window and seeing the miniature houses, cars and trucks. They look so fake; as though I were watching an episode of Mr. Rodger's Neighborhood rather than looking out a window.

6:49pm- Haven't met up with my team yet and the plane is already delayed an hour. Sitting in the Dallas airport doing what I do not enjoy, waiting. It seems as though I have been waiting for this trip for almost a year now, and now that it is here, it continues to get farther and farther away. I keep expecting to wake up and realize that I still have a month until it is time to go.

I've been standing on one verse lately; Mark 11:24 NIV, "Whatever you ask for in prayer, believe that you have received it, and it will be yours."

This verse helps to constantly remind me that it isn't always that God says no, but it could be that I am lacking faith in His powers and grace. This idea of not believing makes me laugh though because I have witnessed, with my own eyes, the Lord do MIGHTY things not only in my own life but in the lives of those around me. God is so amazing, and is able to do far above anything we can ever imagine. We say that we know that and that we believe that, but wow, it still makes me speechless when He comes through and does far greater things than I could even make up in my head.

I spoke with my father on the phone this morning, and his words brought tears to my eyes. He said that he and my mother were excited for my trip. Those were some of the most amazing words that I could have ever heard. I have felt their resistance for this trip since I first mentioned it, and even hid how serious I was about it until it was too late for them to do anything about it. I understand their concerns with my health, but followed God's calling for me to go on this trip. I know God will protect me as well as my team, because we have asked for it in prayer, so it shall be done!

Day Two
Tuesday

6:45 am- Last night was an experience to say the least. We left Dallas two to three hours late and didn't get into Florida until 1:30am. The group was headed to the hotel. I originally had an airport buddy. Instead of paying the extra money and have to go through security again, we were just going to spend the night in the airport, seeing how it was only a matter of hours between flights. He ended up not coming on the trip, which I was not aware of until late yesterday. Even though my airport buddy was not here, I decided to try and tough it out for one evening, so that I wouldn't have to fork over another hundred dollars or so for only a few hours of rest. After about ten minutes of a weird guy staring at me, and following me after I moved, I called Paul, the leader of the trip, and asked for directions to the hotel. They actually hadn't left yet so they waited where they were until I made it that way.

I ended up bunking with Eric and Cathy, a couple on the trip, who had an extra bed in their room. I wasn't planning on sleeping in a bed so I didn't pack anything other than my contact things, so I took out my contacts, and crawled into bed with my jeans on and all. It seemed as though just as I fell asleep, the wake up call came! The call was set for 4:30 in the morning. Yowzers!!

The morning ran rather smoothly, especially considering none of us had more than three hours of sleep. I was not overly tired, which is surprising seeing how I only had about two and a half hours of sleep, and in all actuality, probably less than that.

We are on the plane now, and a few of us even got moved up to first class! Hello leg room! ☺

I am so excited to see what God is doing in Haiti. I was reading Compassion Magazine last night (Summer 2010, Vol. 4, No. 2) and found an interesting statistic about January twelfth's earthquake which killed more than 220,000 people and injured 300,000 more. The magazine also pointed out that a stronger earthquake, which took place in 1994 in Los Angeles CA took only 60 lives that is in a location that is five times as populated. Their claim is that it was not the earthquake's fault it caused so much damage, but rather the country's poverty that produced such grand numbers. Houses, buildings, and towns in general were and are poorly built with cheap materials, which makes disasters such as this one far greater and more devastating. It breaks my heart to think that money, the item that seems to make the world go round, is what is holding a country such as Haiti back. I am excited to see though the country's resilience which I have heard so much about. It seems to me that when you have so little, something as big as Jesus is even bigger. If only we could all forget about money and politics, and go back to the more primitive days when you say "Jesus is all I need" and actually mean it whole heartedly. I cannot wait until everyone is gathered together and only relying on God.

I pray that God uses my team to "show Christ's love through

healing bodies and souls," as the Hospitals of Hope slogan claims. God you are so good! As we are flying with the rising sun, you rise to Your throne and Your mercies are new every morning. I thank You and praise You for this experience. Thank You for the boldness that this week will take. Lord, my life is Yours alone. This week is Yours. Use me as You wish with Your perfect will.

4:00pm- We have settled into the guest quarters at the orphanage! God has definitely been with us. When we arrived at the Port au Prince Airport, we circled over and over, attempted landing twice, and then finally made it on our third try. The pilot mentioned that if we hadn't made it then, we would have had to fly to the Dominican Republic, which really would have messed with our plans. But thankfully we landed, and safely at that.

A view from the airplane of Haiti.

Immigration and Customs was a breeze, but baggage claim was a pure nightmare. It took a good hour or more to get everyone's luggage, and then find the rest of our group members whom we were meeting there and then find their luggage. It was an interesting and hot few hours, that is for sure.

After that we went outside and waited around for "Biggie" to arrange our ride. The ride was most over all crazy. People do not follow the same street rules as we do in the United States. Rules that I enjoy and wish Haiti taught their drivers were ones such as; stay on your own side of the road, don't pass on the left, and whatever you do don't honk at or make obscene comments to pass then go thirty over the speed limit to a cop car, while in front of the police station. To say the least, the ride was quite entertaining, even though there were a few times that I was quite certain we might die! If I would have had to drive from the Airport to our location, we still, to this day, would be sitting in the airport parking lot! Yikes!

We were in two vehicles, I was in the lap of luxury and rode in a semi-air conditioned car, along with three other lucky people. Everyone else rode in a Tap Tap. I am sure it was a fun experience, and one that I later got to have for myself.

The tap tap.

The driver showed us many things but basically just drove around the city of Port au Prince. We saw normal everyday life, but more often than that we witnessed the destruction from the earthquake. It was ridiculous! Still, eight months later, almost to the day, buildings were still as they were the day after the quake. Some buildings look as though they could topple at any moment. Trash was laying everywhere. People were still excavating the city, the buildings, the ruins. They were still looking for missing loved ones. It was heart breaking. The presence of the United Nations was large. We asked Richard, our driver, how he felt about the United Nations being there and he openly told us how much he disliked it.

We even visited what used to be the government buildings, as well as the Presidential Palace. That is where we met our first group of begging children. One even pointed to a camera, smiled, and grabbed my leg in a hug and turned my attention towards the camera. I asked Cathy if she could take a picture. It was breathtaking. These kids were begging to be kids, to run around, to be boys. Instead they quickly remembered what they were there to do and started begging for money claiming that they were hungry. As we climbed into the vehicles, their faces and hands were pressed to the side of the window, still begging. They knew that if they went home empty handed, there would be consequences. It broke my heart to turn away from these kids without providing something for them. We have so much, and they so little, and yet we have nothing that we could give them. We hadn't exchanged any money, and we did not have a grand access of food. All we could do was drive away and pray for them.

A view of the President's Palace.

We drove out of the city, and onto equally poor roads. At one point we slammed to a halt as four goats ran out in front of the vehicle. In the process I hurt my hand pretty well. Only me! Hoping it feels better in the morning. We came up to the bottom of "Goats Mountain," and stopped for a beautiful photo opportunity.

There were so many tents on the side of the mountain. People had relocated themselves there after the earthquake and created their own little village, on the side of the mountain. It amazed me how it seemed that we could not pass an eighth of a mile without seeing lots of people. There are people everywhere. Some selling, some pawning, some sitting, some wandering without an evident purpose, while others were begging for food or money. Most of all, they were starring at this group of white people with their eyes wide open and their mouths open. As I don't know their language, I smiled at the ones that I made eye contact with, and just wondered what they thought of these American invading their land. I hope they not only saw my sympathy but also the hope that my Lord has to offer. I've already had a "God talk" with a Haitian who is a Christian. He is a very talented artist, and spoke English quite well. If we make it back downtown, I hope to buy one of his paintings. Love was shinning out of his eyes. I am still sitting back, playing things safe, putting my feelers out there, but some people are just starring with wide looks of disbelief on their faces as though the earthquake were just a ploy made up for relief efforts. We definitely discovered that it was real, a little too real. The part that amazed me was that these people could not run away from their grief. They must face it over, and over, and over.

Everyday since January twelfth, it is a living reminder for them of how bad things are. They may have thought that things were bad before, but there is no thinking now, things are definitely bad. The good news is that there is hope. They are slowly beginning to clear a few piles of debris, one shovel full at a time. I even saw two new buildings being constructed during our trip, and that right there is a great ray of hope for the Haitian people.

Rubble after January's earthquake

As we drove up Goat Mountain, we drove up a paved road. Praise God for that. Paul, our leader, said it was new since he was last here. It was the windiest road that I have ever been on, times ten, but at least it was paved. I thought of my mom as we went up the mountain because she does not fair well on winding driving passages, she would have had to pass on this one. The view from the top was amazing to say the least though. We also worked our way down the mountain, past tents and tents filled with people. I am not sure why, but I never imagined the amount of people that were there.

Once we arrived at the bottom of the mountain, we passed through one more town before we arrived at the orphanage. It s a very cute building with kids everywhere. Some were playing some sort of tag game, others playing basketball on their very nicely paved court, while others were no where to be seen. We were shown to our rooms and are now waiting for the people staying at the hotel to get back so we can eat dinner and then crash. We are all so exhausted, I can only assume that it will be an early bedtime. Clinics start tomorrow, which I am very excited about.

We had a delicious dinner, but I only picked at it. I wasn't too hungry from all of the excitement. I went back and got my things for a shower and then went over to the orphanage bathroom to shower. I had a nice little surprise during my shower too! A little girl kept popping her head into my shower. It was too funny! After a cleansing shower that semi rejuvenated me, I headed back to the orphanage to see what the kids were up to. There was another group there working with the orphans who I quickly made friends with. They were having a dance party for the kids, which I sat around and watched. It was adorable! I was already in love with these little children! As I sat a few kids left the circle of dancing and came and sat with me. It was rather endearing.

Michelle dancing with the orphans.

A beautiful smile.

⌒◣ Day Three ◢⌒
Wednesday

We saw 288 people at the clinic today! Wow. The patience and resilience of the Haitian people is amazing. Some people sat for hours, or stood, in the heat, just for Motrin. No one even complained, even though it was hot. Our clinic today was at the orphanage, in the church.

We started off the morning at 7:30 with a breakfast of pancakes, omelet looking things, and fried plantains. We even had maple sugar. After breakfast we organized the six large Rubbermaid tubs that the Wheatland Missions group brought with them full of medical supplies and medicines. We also met with a pastor/doctor that has been running a clinic nearby who allowed us to use all of his materials and medicines while we were in Haiti for the week. We all manned our stations and the craziness began. It was definitely organized chaos but chaos none the less.

Haitians waiting to be seen.

People first lined up after signing in with one of the Haitians who recorded their name and number on a piece of paper. They then started to file into the church and sat on the benches to wait to be seen. The first step in the process brought them to Sarah and a translator who filled out a little green slip of paper which showed their name, age, and chief complaint. After that was filled out, they moved over to get their blood pressure and pulse taken and recorded on the same green sheet. They then had to wait on benches until a doctor or nurse was ready to see and diagnose them. The doctor wrote the treatment down and sent them to the pharmacy area for medication distribution. That is mainly where I came into the picture, seeing how I have so much pharmaceutical experience, or not! At any rate, after the first ten patients or so we really had a system down. Even two of the girls from the other group came to help us in the pharmacy, which was amazing as it gave us much needed breaks for water, sitting, or picture taking in my case. What an amazing process. We may not have had a lot of work with what we had numerous times the power would go out, meaning our lights and fans didn't work. They were never really off for more than fifteen or twenty minutes at a time, but with that many people packed in a room, the fans were crucial. It was awesome how everyone worked together and no one complained. Sure, there were the occasional jokes about how hot or tired we were but everyone remained in good moods. Around one, I was finally able to take a break and have a ham sandwich downstairs with everyone. It was so funny because there was a baby kitten who came into the room where the table for breakfast, lunch, and dinner for the staff was during every meal. He and I became buds. He even sat on my lap for a little while. It made me miss my own kittens.

Holding a precious baby.

After lunch I ended up taking a lot more breaks. The long days began wearing on me. I could not believe that it was Wednesday already. The days were flying by. There were so many children that I wanted to take home with me. They were all so cute. I took a couple of them to hold while their parents were getting their blood pressure taken or their parents were being seen by a doctor. The moms were nice and handed them over but kept a close eye on me. It astounded me of how many women, at one time, would be breastfeeding, in the same room. You could look up into the crowd at any given time and find at least six women with their breasts out feeding their child.

Crystal, a girl from the other team, took care of a few nasty wounds, and I was put to the task of helping her and taking pictures. It was rather disgusting. Some of the people we saw should have been seen weeks ago, or even just been putting antibiotic ointment and a Band-Aid on it, which for me seems silly that something that is so easily dispensable in America, is a almost non existent to the Haitian people. When wounds are not treated properly right away however, they can become oozing, festering sores that can cause a lot of pain and unnecessary problems. We saw quite a few people with these problems. They came in saying that their foot hurt, when it fact it was surprising that they were still able to walk with Crocs on their feet in the heat all day long with these pains.

One girl who came to the clinic that day was twelve and had a son who was one. I could not even put myself into her place. When I was eleven, never in a million years had I thought about having my own child to care for. I was worried about clothing, music, and movies. What a different world children are in these days, and maybe even more in remote places like the villages of Haiti. I would have loved to have had the time to sit down with her and hear her story. I would have loved to have sat down and talked with so many of these people. Unfortunately, there was not enough time in the day, or enough translators to help, to have the time to hear people's stories.

The translators that we did have were amazing though. They worked so hard all day. The process would have been so much more efficient if we had spoke their language, but we did pretty well with using translators. It was amusing how easily we fit in with our translators. They were so easy going, and a joy to be around.

We ended the day's clinic at 5:00pm and saw 288 patients that day, well 290 if you include the two workers that were also seen. Dinner was pretty good that night. My favorite part was this brown bean sauce to put on the rice. It was delicious. I was trying very hard to try the majority of the things that were put out for us, and surprisingly enough, I liked most of it. The pickled coleslaw was where I drew the line and did not have more than once. It was so spicy. At dinner that night, the kitten jumped into Doug's lap and enjoyed a nice little nap. Apparently he had a hard day too and needed some rest.

After dinner and some small talk, I headed back to the room and ended up having a very nice talk with the girls about the day and the experience so far. It was neat, to say the least, to hear everyone's perspectives as we all came from different parts of the world and different parts of our own lives.

⌁ Day Four ⌁
Thursday

378 people were seen at the clinic today. We started off late due to part of the crew going to the other clinic and the pharmacy to get more supplies such as Tylenol and antacids. After breakfast we were on a stall tactic and it gave me a great chance to talk with and play with some of the kids. Khara even had a chance to braid one of the little girl's hair for her. It was really, really cute. I had a lot of fun with one little orphan in particular that morning. Bob enjoyed playing with my camera and taking pictures of different people that were walking by. We had a tickle war for a little while and then just sat together and talked with the girls for a while as well.

Eventually it was time to leave so we headed for a walk down the long, steep driveway to the orphanage. The tap tap we were going to take could not make it up the hill without any weight in it, so we had to go to it. We met some of the most random of animals on our walk down the hill such as a cow, donkey, roosters, a horse, and goats. When we got to the bottom of the hill, we discovered that it was very muddy, and had to find a path to go down to get to the road and the tap tap. I won't lie, I was a bit scared to jump down across this puddle, but ended up making it, but almost got hit by a crazy motorized scooter in the process.

Starting the morning braiding some hair.

When we got there, we unloaded the tap tap, well the men unloaded the tap tap, and we began to set up. We set the pharmacy area up in the back of the church. We were very fortunate to take Michelle and Krystel with us again today. They mainly helped in the pharmacy. It was very sweet, Pastor Eli, the pastor of the church, started the day off with a prayer and by leading everyone in the song Blessed Assurance. It brought tears to my eyes to see these people, some of which were laying on the floor, who had walked miles and been waiting for hours, sing to their Savior a love song of peace. It was a great way to start the day.

I love these kids.

Gathering before the clinic started singing Blessed Assurance.

As we were setting up, we noticed three little windows that were behind the pharmacy counting counter, and quickly noticed three little faces in each of them. All day long, there was a kid standing outside the church, looking into one window or another, checking out what we were doing. One of the boys asked what my name was, a common English phrase learned in school. Of course I told him and asked him, and his counterparts their names. They seemed to have a much easier time learning my name than I did theirs. Quickly I would have to get back to work, and would hear my name being said. It was a very heartwarming sound! Try as I might, it was very hard to ignore them and keep on working. I tried my best but usually gave up eventually and went to talk to them for a little while before quickly returning back to work. It definitely kept a smile on my face as I worked throughout the day.

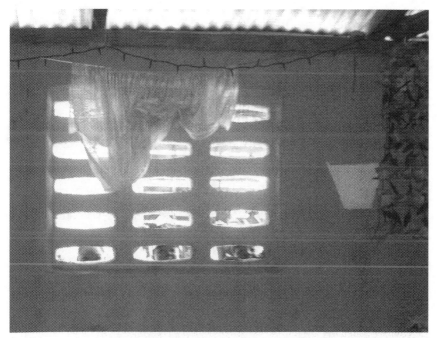

Children looking in the windows.

Another exciting part of the day was the use of a potty tent! On the way over, in the tap tap, someone had asked Marcus, one of the interpreters, what the bucket was for, and he laughed and only said, "oh, you'll see!" He had such a smile on his face when he said it that we were all very curious. Later on we found out exactly what it was for. When a convenient looking lid was placed on it, it became our hover potty. They even had a fold up potty tent to put around it for some privacy. It was quite amusing to watch the Haitian's faces when one of us went into the tent as they seemed to just squat wherever they could. One of us would disappear into the tent, and come back out and they were curious as all get out. It almost made it even stranger as when you came out, there was a decent group of onlookers.

One of my favorite parts of the day revolved around the

windows near the pharmacy area. There was a little boy holding what I assumed was his little sister. I found time to play peek-a-boo with them as much as possible. They were by far, the cutest children that I had found so far in Haiti. The boy stood there, holding his sister to the window, for a few hours. Once some of our helpers recovered a bit from the heat, I went outside for a bit and grabbed one of our translators at the same time. I was able to talk to the boy and found out that yes indeed he was holding his little sister. His mom let him leave the house to see the Americans if he took her with him. I asked him if he went to the church we were at, and he said no. So I asked him if he was a Christian, to which he replied, "I don't know." I then continued to question him if he knew Christ, if he believed Christ died to save his soul, you know the typical things. It was a slow process as it had to be translated, and there were tears intermixed by myself, the boy, and the translator. We had hit a wall at some point, and eventually he said that he had to steal and he knew God did not approve so he did not want to say he was a Christian when God could not love him because he had to steal food. I explained that if he wanted me to pray with him and ask for forgiveness, and then just ask God to provide for him that God would do that, if he believed. There was much more crying and eventually I left his side, with him being back in the right sight of the Lord. I spent a lot of time that day thinking about him and praying that God would do something miraculous for him. Later that evening, he showed up again, this time without his sister. He held up his hand and in it was an entire loaf of bread. The smile on his face was larger than I thought was even possible. He held up his finger, as if to tell me to hold on, and ran the other way. He came back a few minutes later with one of our translators who told me that he was proud to come show me what he had. When he got home, someone had given his family bread and meat for dinner. He said he had to go because he just ran out of the house and his mom would be worried about the bread. I just stood there with the translator in awe. I shouldn't have been, I should have known that God would provide, but it was so quick that it amazed me. I am so proud of God's power! I also love that I never grow tired of what He is doing in people's lives. God is so amazing!

One of my favorite pictures.

There were even times when it got a little tense in that church. Some of the people had been waiting for hours to see someone. It was hot, not to mention most of the people that were there were there for a medical reason. At one point one of the men tried to cut in line which caused a bit of a ruckus. Our translators once again came to the rescue and quickly explained that if they were loud or causing problems that they would have to leave without seeing a doctor, at least that is what the translators told us they said.

It was a long and hot day, but definitely had it's rewarding moments. When we stopped for lunch for fifteen minutes in the middle of the day, it was interesting to see some local village people standing on a hill nearby just looking to see what we were up to. Not only were we taking a break and eating, but some of us were using the potty tent, and had our cameras out taking pictures of the beautiful countryside. It was relaxing, and felt amazing to just sit and relax and enjoy some of God's creation for a few minutes.

Haitians watching from the hill.

Since we had a late start, and because there were so many people, we realized that we were not going to be able to treat everyone that was there to see a doctor. It was very discouraging once we realized what we were going to have to do, and it definitely broke down our spirits at least up in the pharmacy where I was. We only had a few flashlights, and it was very hard to see what we were doing and for the doctors to also see what they were doing. With the sun coming up so early in the day, it also goes down early in the day, and although we were tired, hot, and hungry, we were not interested in turning away people; however, we had no choice.

Sarah, one of the people that was in our group, had a great idea to at least send everyone off with something, even if they were not able to see a doctor. She created goodie bags including vitamins and pain relievers for everyone. It felt good that they at least did not have to go home empty handed, although it still was not fun watching the interpreters explaining why they were not going o be seen. No one seemed overly angry by any means, just disappointed.

When we got back to the orphanage that night, there were a few members of the team who felt very discouraged. They didn't feel like we were doing enough and didn't know if it was worth our troubles to come all this way. Other members of the team, including myself, reminded others of what we were doing there as well as the big picture of what we were doing. It was not always about curing their problems, but sometimes about listening and giving them hope for tomorrow.

One of our team members was getting ready for bed that night and found ants in her luggage. They were so small, but in everything! We even lost power while she was trying to clean out her suitcase. It was definitely an adventure.

 Day Five
Friday

The information provided for today is based off of what I was told by others as well as the pictures that I have as I do not remember much of what happened on Friday due to an accident.

We woke up this morning and two local ladies had set up a market at the orphanage for us. They had different types of souvenirs and clothing. It was really sweet. I bought a painting by a local artist and some cloth bookmarks that were embroidered. Some people bought swords, statues, jewelry, and jewelry boxes that were carved. There were even tablecloths and clothing that were embroidered. The ladies had some scrubs embroidered as well. They said that they have medical groups a lot and so they are good sellers.

Local women made a market for us to shop at.

After everyone had a chance to eat breakfast and shop at the market, we got ready to leave for our next clinic. We took everything with us because we were spending the next two nights in a different city. It was our first day with internet access as well! We all huddled around one of the boy's computers to use the internet. I was excited to be able to send an email to my family, letting them know that everything was going well.

We had an interesting drive to our next clinic and even had to get out of the tap tap because we got stuck in the mud. It took a lot of men to push us out, but eventually we could get back into the vehicle. The clinic was held at another church, and there were so many people waiting for us when we got there. At the end of the clinic, we had to walk our supplies to the tap tap a ways down the road because they did not want the tap tap to get stuck again.

It had been raining a lot of the day so it was very muddy, and it even started raining while we were walking, which made for an adventure, By the time we got back to the tap tap it was dark and we started our way to Pastor Claude's in Hinche.

Haitians waiting outside the church.

On the way, we hit some holes in the "road" and I ended up catching some air, hitting my head on a metal bar, and passing out. Apparently, Eunji noticed I was missing from sitting next to her and had them stop the tap tap, meanwhile one of the doctors jumped across the medical supplies sitting in the middle of the truck bed, and tried to get me conscious. After two minutes, they were able to get me to open my eyes and had me lay down on the bench of the tap tap. They called to the other truck ahead and had them come back, at which point I changed places with one of them and sat the rest of the way to Pastor Claude's in the air conditioning. Once we got to Pastor Claude's, I attempted walking to sit inside where the meal was going to be, but had a hard time doing that. I was not in the mood for food so I sat in the corner and tried to go to sleep. One of the doctors kept yelling at me to keep me awake, which I did not appreciate. After they had finished their meals, I went back to the truck and laid down in the front seat so I could sleep. Once we got to the hotel, I quickly got into my bed, with some assistance, and went to sleep. Everyone on the team took turns waking me up every hour or so to make sure that the concussion did not get worse.

As I mentioned, I don't remember any of this, and can only say what I have been told by various members of the team. I am so glad, looking back, that I was with who I was with. They were able to do so much more for me than would have been available had I just been in Haiti with any missions team. I thank the Lord for His wisdom that He gave them and that He kept His hand on me the entire time.

Day Six
Saturday

Today is another of those days that I only remember bits and pieces, but I have heard the story told so many times to different doctors, nurses, team members, and family members, that I can pretty much tell it myself.

Today was the day of our big clinic. It was in Hinge, not far from the hotel we were staying at. Cathy ended up staying behind with me, as she did not get much sleep the night before and I was not allowed to go to the clinic with my team and was supposed to stay behind with someone. Nicholson also stayed behind incase we were in need of a translator for whatever reason. It turns out that that was not a bad idea. I started the day with a shower, which I apparently wanted badly. As I was not stable on my feet, I had to sit in the tub and let the shower water run over my body in order to get clean. Before the team left for the day, Kathryn hooked me up to an IV since I was not staying conscious long enough to drink as much as they really wanted me to be drinking. They also gave me some sort of steroid injection to stop the swelling in my brain faster than my body was doing it on its own.

As far as I am aware, Cathy and I stayed in the hotel room for the day, by ourselves, with little connection to the outside world. She would check on me every so often and answer questions and talk to me when I was semi-lucid, but it sounds like that was not all that often.

Around four o'clock in the afternoon, Cathy was checking on me and I no longer was responding to her questions, pokes, or yells. She got Nicholson to see if he could help and it was not helping. She checked my pupils and my right pupil was fine, but my left pupil was not behaving correctly. It was then that she started to worry. She placed a phone call to the other doctors on the team, who were actually wrapping up their last patients and ended up hopping in a truck and coming back immediately. They tried to wake me up several times and when that was not working, they decided to start working on getting me out of Haiti and back into the United States for medical care that they could no longer provide.

From what I understand, Cathy was looking through some of my things for something, and came across my travel insurance, and it was then that they knew they'd be able to fly me home immediately. Kathryn started the chain of events in a series of phone calls and was able to get a Med Evacuation team to Port au Prince the next morning. More calls were made, as well as decisions, and Kathryn, Cathy, Nicholson, a driver, and I headed to Port au Prince. I hear it was not a smooth car ride at all and that I "should be glad I didn't remember it." I can only imagine seeing how the roads were what they were. We arrived in Port au Prince late in the evening and went to a make shift hospital run by American doctors and nurses. They really couldn't do anything for me other than keep me stable until my flight came in the morning.

Cathy and Kathryn took turns sleeping in a different room while the other one stayed with me. There was not much that I remembered about that night, other than two people dying while I was there. There was a 28 week old baby who died, and an adult who died. It was sad. I sat there wondering if I was going to die there too, and what would happen to me if I did.

God provided me with comfort and with amazing people that were so supportive and so amazing to me. I am so thankful that it was evident that God was with me the entire time. He gave me an amazing testimony to share with others. Even with everything that happened, I am so glad that I was able to go on this missions trip. It was such an amazing experience and I am so thankful for it.

Day Seven
Sunday

Although I didn't sleep much at night, I remember a lot of the hospital that morning. I was moved from the "ER" room into another room. The room had about 12 beds in it, each with very different issues going on. The man I remember the most was an older man, who was wearing a diaper and snoring louder than even my dad snores! It was ridiculous!!! At what must have been 7 or 8 in the morning, a lot of family members started showing up. Apparently in Haiti it is custom for family members to do the daily bathing of their sick or injured loved ones, as well as change their sheets, etc. They do more of the personal care while the doctors and nurses do the medical care. I remarked at one point, to Kathryn or Cathy I'm not sure, that I felt like I should have been getting a sponge bath! Luckily, they did not take that as a hint and start one! One of the women brought water in in an old gasoline jug. It really bothered me, because I don't care how much you clean that jug, there is still going to be gasoline in it! The living circumstances there are despicable, and it is no wonder diseases are spreading a mile a minute. It is unfortunate that there isn't more that we can do, but there are also a lot of problems in the United States that also need to be taken care of before we try and fix the world. It seemed like most Haitians were pretty happy and proud of what they had and how they made things work. It made me laugh, because I know that if I had to bathe out of water from an old gasoline jug, even if I didn't have to walk miles to get it, I would have thrown a fit. It really showed me that you have to be thankful with what you have. Sure my bathroom has been leaking for a month and there is mold growing in it, but what is that compared to someone who has no bathroom but still has the mold? These Haitian people that I either came in contact with or observed taught me so much about not only appreciating what I do have, but also that no matter what your circumstances, God WILL provide. I praise God for that!

At any rate, we eventually got in the car again and headed off to the airport in order to get on the plane. That 5 minute drive turned into what felt like four hours, although I honestly have no idea how long it actually took. During the ride I was getting so agitated because I didn't feel good and I was in pain and they kept telling me we were almost there, but we weren't. I remember finally finding an entrance to the executive part of the airport, getting out of the car, which was a struggle in and of itself, and going in. I went through a silly pat down and my luggage went through security and we watched as small jets landed and took off, with no word of where our plane was. I dozed for a while because my head was hurting so bad, and eventually we went back to the car because apparently the plane was at the other end of the airport and could not get through to where we were. There was more driving around, and more dozing off, I woke up a few times to people being frustrated, getting in and out of the car, slamming doors, etc. but I just went back to sleep. The next time I woke up

I was told we were at immigration, which was a tent that could probably comfortably sleep four grown men. Eventually we found the plane and crew members. By that time I was pretty much out of it and I really remember about getting on the plane was that I thought that they were going to drop the stretcher.

I have been told I had a rough flight due to the fact that I didn't want to lay down, and I really wanted water, but was not allowed any, even though they were giving Cathy some. I don't remember any of the flight, which is too bad because it is going to be the most expensive flight that I have ever been on, and will ever be on. There were two paramedic like people, one person noting everything that was happening, a pilot, copilot, Cathy, and myself on the plane.

We landed at the Ft. Lauderdale Airport and went through customs and immigration, none of which I remember, and then got into an ambulance with a ton of other people. I remember not liking the ambulance, or being in the ambulance, but that is about it. I have been told that I tried to break free of the ambulance many times, some while it was still moving and others while it was at a traffic light. Apparently the paramedics were using the word "sedation" quite a bit. At any rate, we made it to the hospital, and I did not have to be sedated. I was checked into the ER, they even already had a room ready for me. Now that is what I call service. There were masses of doctors around me, asking me questions, most of which I looked to Cathy for. I hadn't remembered the accident or most of what had happened in the past 30 plus hours and so was no good to them. Before I knew it, my dad was even there. He and Cathy asked me many, many questions, and I couldn't figure out why they wouldn't just let me sleep. That was all I wanted to do, take some pain medication and sleep. But that is definitely not something that is allowed at the hospital. They are always poking, prodding, or questioning. I had an x-ray done, a CT scan, as well as urine and blood tests.

After many doctors, nurses, and other people whom I could not identify came in, I eventually was taken upstairs to check into my room, 825. Once I was up there the questioning began again. I was brought a "late dinner" so I'd assume it was somewhere between six and eight at that time. My dad and Cathy stayed for a while to make sure I was okay, and then my dad took her to the hotel to get a nice hot shower, which I was envious of, and to get some much needed sleep.

After they left, a nurse came in and started doing something that I found very strange and unenjoyable. Apparently it is customary to take pictures of all of your bruises, all over your body, when you check in to a hospital. This was a practice that I was not familiar with and did not enjoy, however, I was offered a copy of the pictures when I left on Tuesday, I turned that offer down pretty quickly!

I didn't sleep so well that night, all they were giving me for pain was Tylenol, which I did not feel was helping. I was not a fan of being woken up after I finally did fall asleep, every few hours. I suppose it goes along the same lines as the saying everyone's mom always said, "when you're under my roof, you'll follow my rules." Apparently being woken up at midnight, four, and eight were a part of hospital rules.

God was definitely present that night. He was obviously always present, but he was in a more tangible presence that night than I had felt before. I kept waking up to someone special in my room. The first time it was my mom's voice, her hand brushing lightly through my hair, telling me she loved me. My grandpa visited my room that night too and laid in bed with me until I fell asleep, with his hand entangled in mine while reading me some of his favorite Bible scriptures.

⟿ Day Eight ⟿
Monday

Monday I awoke to some horrid breakfast that they actually expected me to eat, and soon after Cathy and my dad were back. It was nice to have them in the room, even though I was dozing off and on the majority of the time, just knowing they were there was amazing. Cathy left at one point for lunch and came back with the cutest gift I have gotten in a long time. It was a stuffed bear, with bandadges stitched onto his head, on the right side just like where my pain was. He was in a hospital gown, the back of which showed his bum, and on his hospital gown it said, "Get Better Beary Soon." He was a major source of comfort while I was in the hospital for those few days, especially when I was alone and feeling crummy.

Saying goodbye to Cathy was very hard to do, especially since she was like my mom for the past few days, she was who I looked for when I woke up to make sure things were okay, and it was hard to say goodbye to her, knowing that I don't have the money to go visit anytime soon! This all could have turned out so much differently if it wasn't for her and the medical team that I was with and their fast acting medical effort. They had me on prayer chains across the country before I was even conscious enough to understand how badly I was hurt. I am so thankful that God provided me with that motherly comfort while I was away. Even through texts after she left, she reminded me that God was in control and to continue seeking Him during this hard time.

My dad had to leave to take Cathy back to the airport, so I said goodbye, had one more picture taken of us, and was once again all alone. I had a bit of an emotional breakdown shortly after they left. I did not understand why all of this had happened and why God wouldn't let me finish what I had started. It was clear later on that I was able to touch doctors, nurses, and technicians, as well as random people at the airport, with my story, in a strong way that apparently needed to be done. Did God cause the injury? Of course not! But He did allow it to happen, and then quickly, once I was back inside the United States, healed my body in order to show His miracle working power to others. He was using me in any capacity to show his love to others, through this rough time.

I was soon taken to get an MRI and a VRI to try and catch anything that the CT scan could have missed. I was in the loud machine for over an hour, which was not fun at all. Eventually though, I was taken back to my room. Apparently the doctor that was in charge of my case came to my room while I was in CT scan, and promised to come back later. He was the guy I was looking for, because I couldn't have any pain medication until he cleared it, needless to say, I was ready to see him!

My dad came back later that night and worked on things for work, as it was a work day for him, and he was behind due to his unexpected travel arrangements. I did a lot of off and on sleeping that afternoon and evening, but really just wanted to take some pain medication. I suppose God was showing me patience or something, because in a hospital that large, I did not understand why I couldn't get something stronger than Tylenol.

I was able to get my first American shower that night! I was so excited! I had asked my nurse if I could take a shower and she said yes, but that she needed to wrap my arm first so water did not get into my IV. She straightened my arm, and wrapped a clear trash bag around my arm and taped it down good with of course the tape that I'm allergic to, but at that point, I didn't even care, I wanted a shower. I got in the bathroom, got undressed, which was a process in and of itself, and got in the shower. I tried for over 10 minutes to get warm water to come out of that shower, because that was all that I wanted, but the thermometer near the handle never went above 70 degrees. Frustrated, I took yet another cold shower. I had forgotten how hard it was to shower one armed, as I could not bend my left arm at all due to the trash bag and tape (I found out the next morning, through my dad, that there was indeed hot water but that I had started turning the handle the wrong direction!). Once I was dressed and back in bed I called my nurse to undo the tape job, which was painful. My dad, on the other side of the room was even wincing and closing his eyes, not helpful dad! ☺

The rest of the night was uneventful. I was able to call my mom and talk to her for a little bit, which made me happy, and eventually fell asleep. As you probably have figured out by now, that doctor did not stop back into my room later that night!

⌒ᴧ Day Nine ᴧ⌒
Tuesday

Tuesday was a crazy, crazy day. I awoke to my father having a pretty heated conversation with then nurse manager, I later found out, about where this doctor was. I had already been signed off to be discharged by all of my other doctors and was just waiting on this one doctor to sign off and discharge me so that we could choose a flight and head home. This "head doctor" had never even seen me, so the fact that he was holding up pain medication and now my discharge was ridiculous. Had it not been for my father, I would probably still be there in the hospital, four days later. I am not sure as to how many people he actually spoke with, but eventually, he talked to the correct set of people in the correct order, and the doctor finally showed up. He walked in as if he knew who I was and what was going on, and as if we were crazy for wanting to leave. My dad calmly explained that every other doctor, that had actually seen me, had already signed off on my discharge and that we were in a holding pattern for tickets, etc. until he signed the papers. He said that since I had not seen a neurologist yet that I could not go. I explained that I had seen this one neurologist numerous times and showed him the business card that I had from him and everything. He left the room, checked on a few things and came back saying that I could go, the neurologist had never put anything in my file about seeing him. Within 15 minutes, my nurse Lio, came in with my discharge papers and went over them with me. He unhooked me from all of the silly monitors, took out my IV and wished me luck. Before we were even packed up and ready to go there was someone there with a wheelchair to take me home. We made a stop at the records department and then I waited outside for my dad to bring around the rental car.

We went to Chili's for lunch, and I tried my best to eat, and not fall asleep at the table. It was frustrating that I was so tired, when all I had been doing for the past few days was sleeping and sitting and sleeping some more. Apparently it is normal after a concussion/contusion and it is just the body's way of giving all of its energy to the brain in order for it to heal, or something like that. Cathy tried to explain it to me, but I'm still having a hard time remembering everything.

My dad showed me around the city, we even stopped at a beach to take pictures, but that was enough for me. As much as I would have loved to play tourist, I was tired, and just wanted to sleep in the car, so we started our drive to the Miami Airport. Dad made a few stops along the way and I decided to stay in the car during them. We eventually showed up at the airport, luckily quite early, and made our way to the ticket counter. Now, what I have not shared, is that my father had been on the phone numerous times before leaving the hospital to change my ticket and they told us specifically that we needed a piece of paper which had proof that I was in the hospital during the time that I was supposed to board my airplane. When we got to the counter, the guy behind the counter told us an altogether different story. He said we needed a piece of paper, on hospital letterhead, in paragraph form, stating that it was "O.K." to fly. At this point, both my father and I were done playing games and just wanted to go home. He agreed to talk to his manager, so we took a seat elsewhere until his manager was available. He came back later saying that his manager agreed that I was not allowed on the airplane until I had a piece of paper from my doctor saying that I was allowed to fly. The pack of 15 plus papers from the hospital were not enough for them, they wanted something very specific filled out and sent in. Now you might be thinking that this isn't a very big deal at all, afterall, doctors fill out papers like that all the time. Well let me remind you that my "head doctor" has been MIA my entire hospital stay, and we left on a rather sour note. My father made a few calls, and of course could only speak to the secretary who said she would pass on the message. The hopes of getting home were fleeing. I began to laugh! I knew it was either that or I would begin to cry, so laugh it was.

A group picture at one of the clinics.

A group of children.

A boy digging through the rubble.

⌇ Afterthoughts ⌇

Haiti was an experience of a lifetime! God was moving through us, onto these people. He was extending His love and choosing to do so through His servants whom He called to preach the Word unto all of the world. What an honor to be able to say, "Yes, Lord. Here I am. Pick me." He could have choose anyone else to go, but He created this team in a way that worked for His riches and glory. Some were doctors, nurses, or medical school students. Others were mechanics and photographers. And then there was a pastor, a pilot, and a school teacher. We were all from different parts of the world, with different talents and gifts, and yet God orchestrated us so that we could fit together and be God's hands to these hurting people of Haiti. Many people asked why I was going on a medical missions trip with no medical experience. In all honesty, I just had to laugh and say, I'm not quite sure, but God said go, so I go. I stepped out in faith and God rewarded that by bringing us all home safely, eventually, and by providing opportunities for us to share His word and love with other people. Working in the pharmacy, I had a chance to pray over every prescription I filled. It was something the doctors and nurses writing the scripts did not have time to do. It was something that I felt I was supposed to do, and I'm trusting that it was worth while. Was the trip exhausting? YES! Was it draining? Yes! Was it the most amazing and powerful trip I've ever been on? YES!!!! God moved through us in so many different ways. He also got a hold of us and changed and shaped our lives. He showed us what it was to be His servant and how to use our skills and passions that He gave us, to serve Him. I originally assumed that I would be staying back at the orphanage and playing with the children. God had a different plan. Someone had to locate and count out the medicines. Someone had to be able to read the rushed, messy handwriting of doctors and nurses. I was able to be that someone. What an amazing feeling to dedicate a week of your life to God. I woke up and didn't worry about not having a job this fall, I didn't worry about what I needed to buy at the store, and I most definitely did not worry about what bills needed to be paid. I woke up and wondered who I would be able to touch today? Who's face could I bring a smile to amidst all of the pain they were going through? Who could I talk to about God, even with language barriers? I've come to realize that God will use any person to spread His love through the valleys and mountains, but only if we are willing. He doesn't need us, yet He chooses to use us. What an awesome feeling of love and honor that creates in my heart every time I think about it.

Hospitals of Hope

Mission:

Hospitals of Hope's mission can be summed up in the phrase "Showing Christ's Love by Healing Bodies and Souls." We accomplish this by improving the healthcare of the under-served in the name of Christ, both in the United States and around the world, through the gathering and distribution of medical supplies, the establishment and support of low-cost clinics and hospitals, and the sending of volunteers and students to serve at our locations abroad.

History and influence:

Hospitals of Hope began when a young physician assistant, Michael Wawrzewski, took a number of short-term mission trips overseas. He was moved to action when he saw that many around the world lack basic medical care and die from easily preventable or treatable diseases such as diarrhea and malaria. He saw an eleven-year-old girl dying of untreated tuberculosis, a farmer with a fractured femur left for dead, and a baby with congenital cataracts—leaving her blind for life.

In 1998, Michael joined with other Wichita, Kansas community members committed to changing the odds of those living without accessible healthcare by founding Hospitals of Hope. Since then, we have sent over 1700 volunteers on short-term trips to provide health care and train local medical staff, and over 100,000 patients have been treated at our clinic and hospital in Bolivia. Countless others have benefited from our work in Liberia and Haiti and from the supplies we have shipped worldwide.